Strings of *praise*

12 Worship Arrangements for
One or More String Players
Arranged by Stan Pethel

CONTENTS

Above All 4

As the Deer 8

Come, Now Is the Time to Worship 12

He Is Exalted ~~18~~

Here I Am to Wo~~rship~~

How Great Is Ou~~r~~

In Christ Alone 36

Jesus, Draw Me Close 40

Lord, I Lift Your Name on High 44

Sanctuary 50

Shine, Jesus, Shine 54

You Are My All in All 60

Shawnee Press, Inc. &

Exclusively Distributed by Hal Leonard Corporation

Visit Shawnee Press Online at www.shawneepress.com/songbooks

PREFACE

Strings of Praise is a companion book to **Winds of Praise**. The two books will work independently or together with any combination of instruments. Unlike **Winds of Praise**, this book was not designed as a stand-alone instrumental project. Strings should be accompanied by the piano part (SB1040) or the CD tracks included with this book.

The solo line can be performed by just about any solo instrument from any part in **Winds of Praise** or **Strings of Praise**.

As with **Winds of Praise**, these arrangements can be played:

> As a solo with piano or CD track.
> In any combination with parts from either book.

They are a good length for preludes, offertories, and instrument features. If a rhythm section is used they can play from the Piano/Score book (SB1040).

The songs are in good "singing" keys if you want to have a group of singers or your congregation join in the performance.

The parts are not difficult and as long as the piano or CD track and a solo part are being played, adding any other instruments on the ensemble parts will just enhance the performance.

I hope you enjoy these arrangements and find them useful in your music ministry. Let us know at Shawnee Press how we can continue to develop products that will be valuable to you (info@shawneepress.com).

Stan Pethel

PUBLICATIONS AVAILABLE:

SB1055 VIOLIN (with CD) $14.95

SB1056 VIOLA / CELLO / STRING BASS (with CD) $14.95

ABOUT THE ARRANGER

DR. STAN PETHEL is a Professor of Music and Chair of Fine Arts at Berry College near Rome, Georgia. He has been on the music faculty at Berry College since 1973. He holds a Bachelor of Music, and Master of Fine Arts degrees from the University of Georgia and a Doctorate of Musical Arts degree from the University of Kentucky. In addition to his duties as Chair of Fine Arts at Berry College Dr. Pethel teaches music theory, composition and arranging, world music, and low brass lessons.

He is a widely published composer and arranger with over 1000 works in publication with 26 different publishers. His writing includes works for choir, piano, organ/piano duet, symphonic band, jazz ensemble, orchestra, hand bells, solo instrument and piano, and various chamber music ensembles.

He is married to Jo Ann Pethel, a pianist and music educator. They have three grown children: Mary Ellen, college history teacher; Rob, a missionary with the International Mission Board; and Joseph, a physical education teacher.

Above All

Viola / Cello / String Bass
ENSEMBLE

Music by **LENNY LEBRANC** *and* **PAUL BALOCHE**
Arranged by **STAN PETHEL**

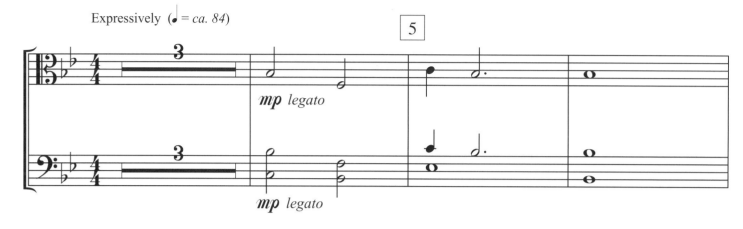

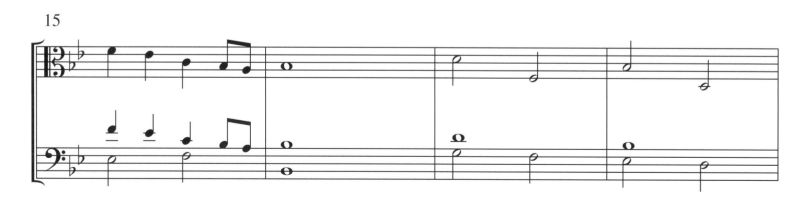

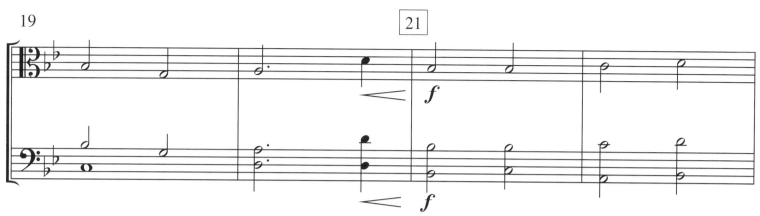

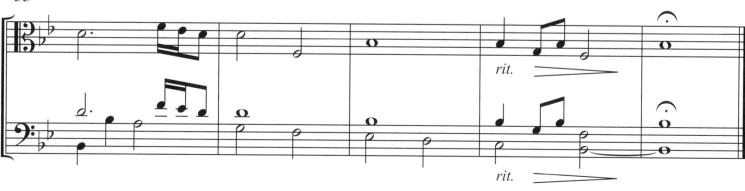

Above All

Viola / Cello / String Bass
SOLO

Music by **LENNY LEBRANC** *and* **PAUL BALOCHE**
Arranged by **STAN PETHEL**

Expressively (♩ = *ca. 84*)

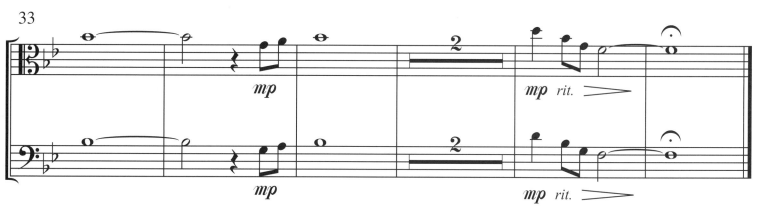

As the Deer

Viola / Cello / String Bass
ENSEMBLE

Music by **MARTIN NYSTROM**
Arranged by **STAN PETHEL**

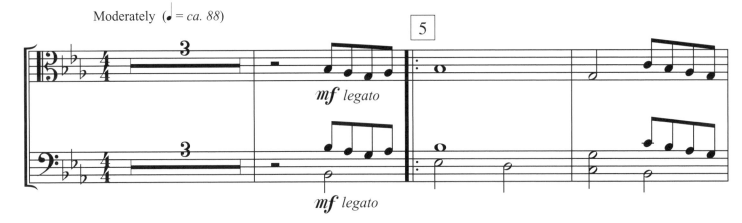

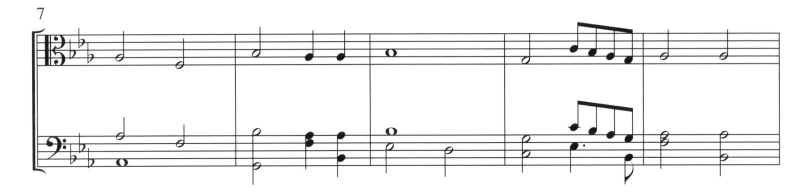

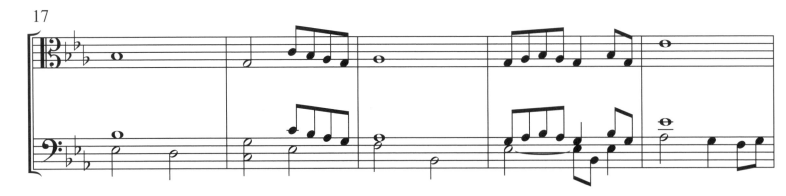

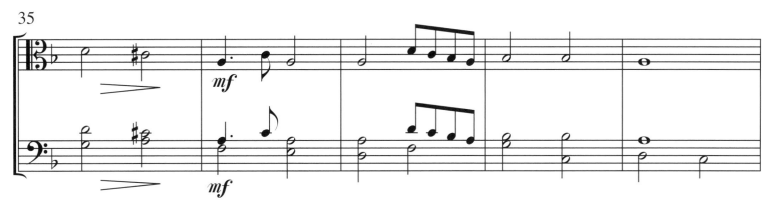

As the Deer

Viola / Cello / String Bass
SOLO

Music by **MARTIN NYSTROM**
Arranged by **STAN PETHEL**

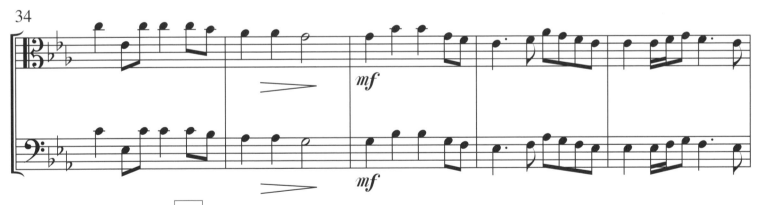

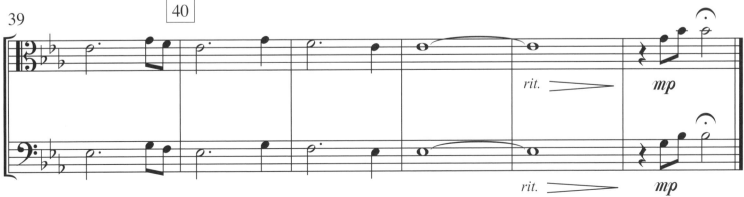

Come, Now Is the Time to Worship

Viola / Cello / String Bass
ENSEMBLE

Music by **BRIAN DOERKSEN**
Arranged by **STAN PETHEL**

Come, Now Is the Time to Worship

Viola / Cello / String Bass
SOLO

Music by **BRIAN DOERKSEN**
Arranged by **STAN PETHEL**

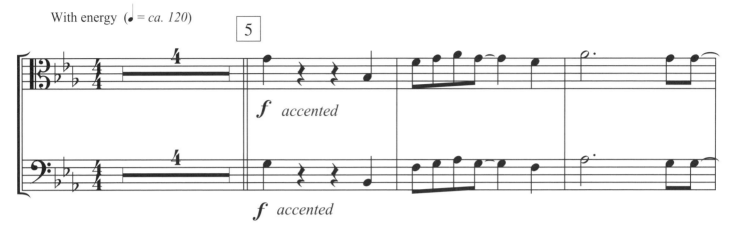

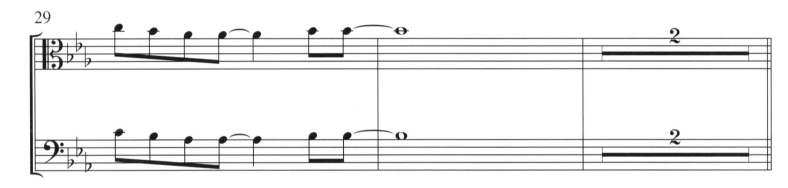

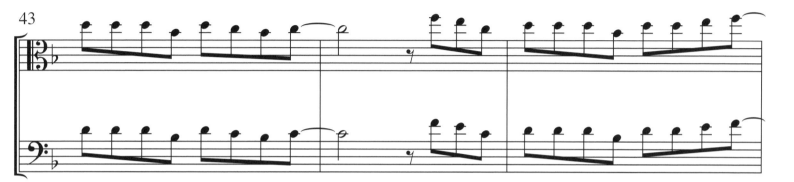

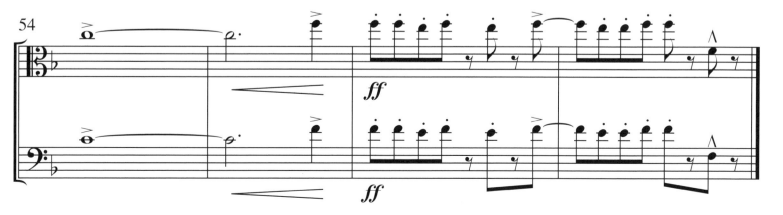

He Is Exalted

Viola / Cello / String Bass
SOLO

Music by **TWILA PARIS**
Arranged by **STAN PETHEL**

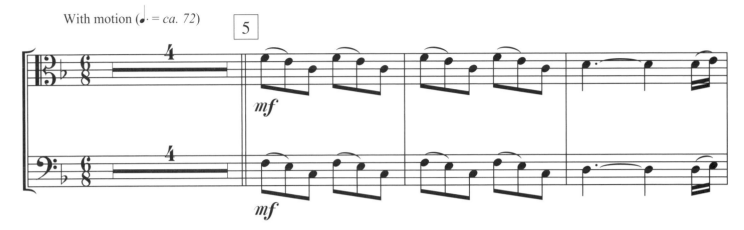

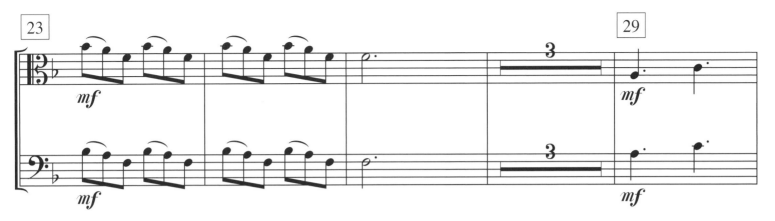

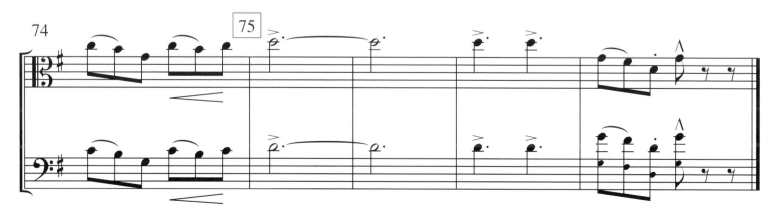

He Is Exalted

Viola / Cello / String Bass
ENSEMBLE

Music by **TWILA PARIS**
Arranged by **STAN PETHEL**

26

31

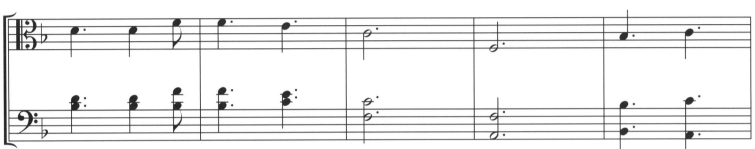

36

37

41

45

46

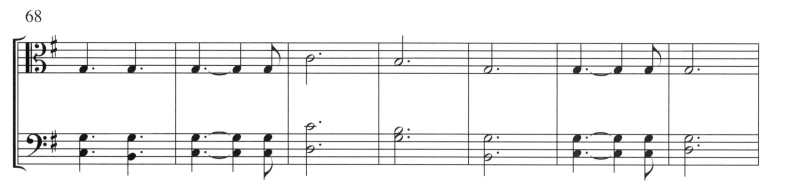

Here I Am to Worship

Viola / Cello / String Bass
ENSEMBLE

Music by **TIM HUGHES**
Arranged by **STAN PETHEL**

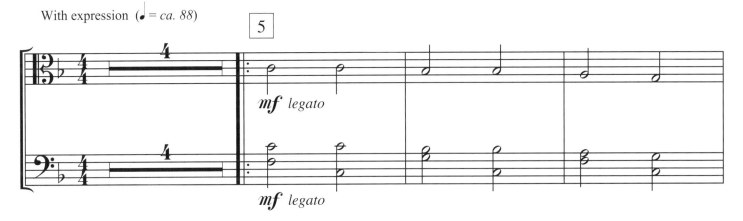

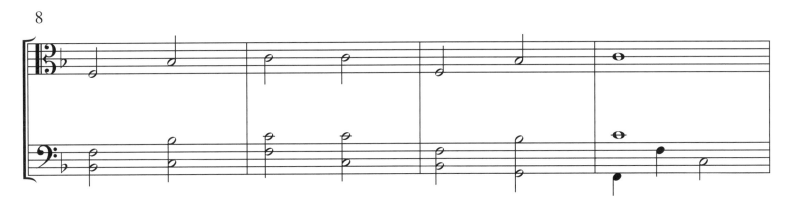

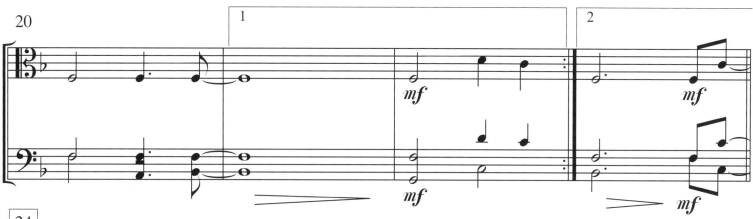

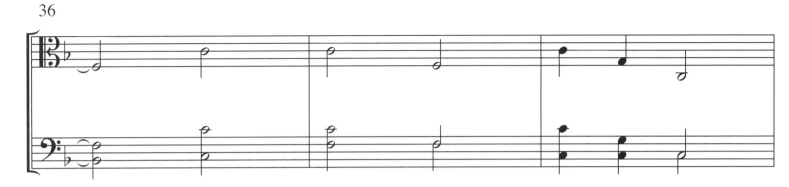

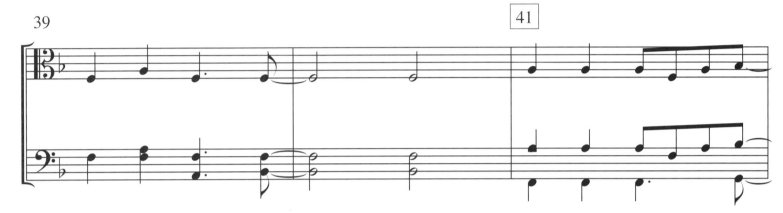

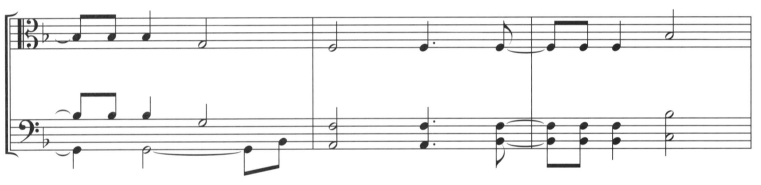

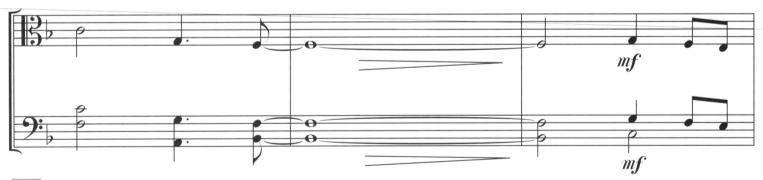

Here I Am to Worship

Viola / Cello / String Bass

SOLO

Music by **TIM HUGHES**
Arranged by **STAN PETHEL**

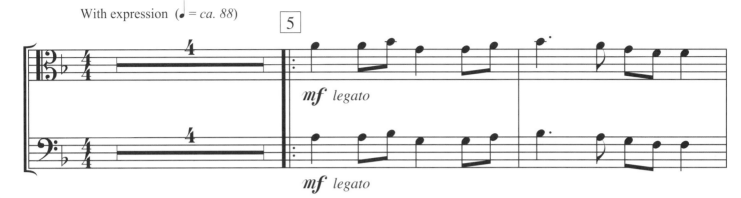

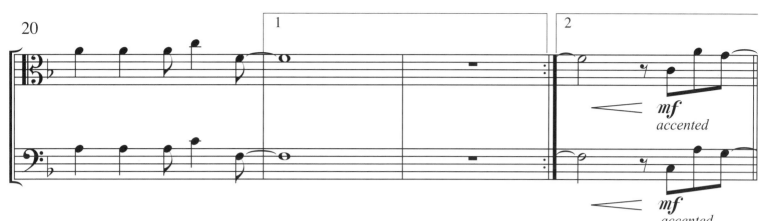

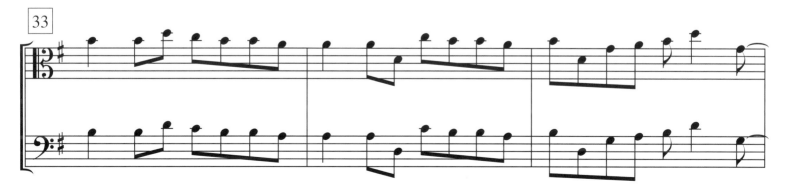

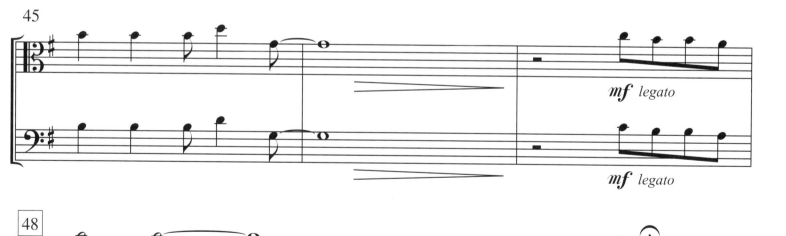

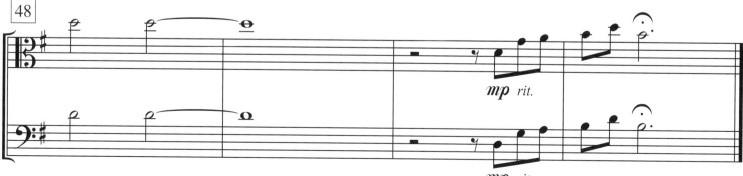

How Great Is Our God

Viola* / Cello / String Bass
ENSEMBLE

Music by **CHRIS TOMLIN,**
JESSE REEVES *and* **ED CASH**
Arranged by **STAN PETHEL**

*Viola double Cello 1

How Great Is Our God

Viola / Cello / String Bass
SOLO

Music by **CHRIS TOMLIN,**
JESSE REEVES *and* **ED CASH**
Arranged by **STAN PETHEL**

Driving Rhythm (♩ = *ca. 112*)

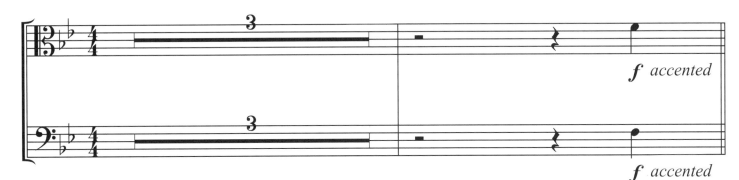

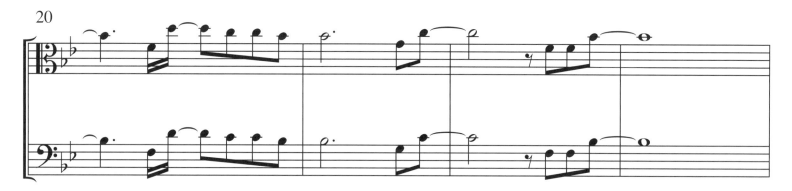

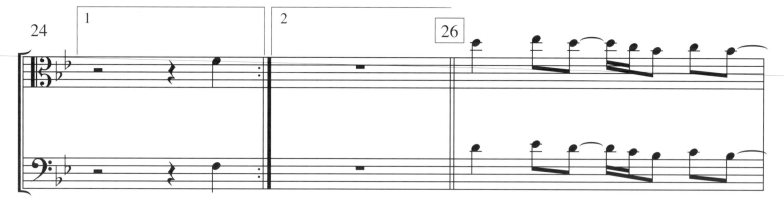

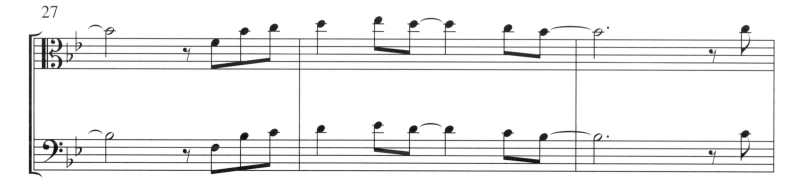

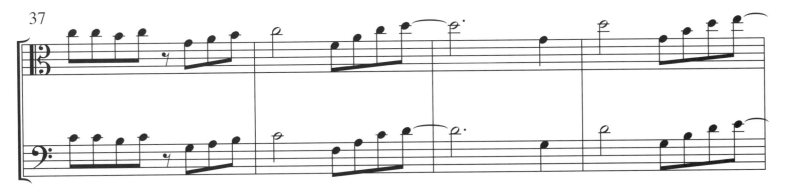

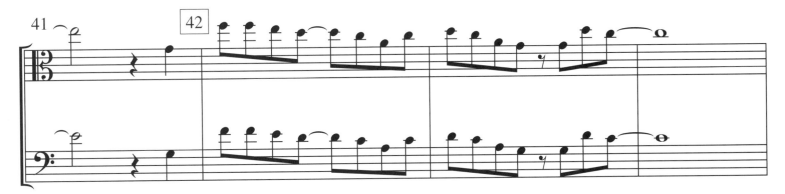

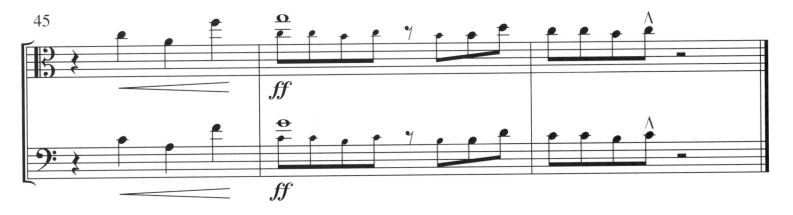

In Christ Alone

Viola / Cello / String Bass
ENSEMBLE

Music by **KEITH GETTY** *and* **STUART TOWNEND**
Arranged by **STAN PETHEL**

25

30 31

35

40 43

45

50

In Christ Alone

Viola / Cello / String Bass
SOLO

Music by **KEITH GETTY** *and* **STUART TOWNEND**
Arranged by **STAN PETHEL**

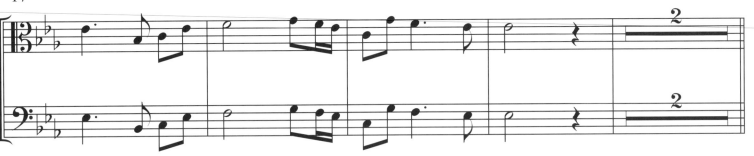

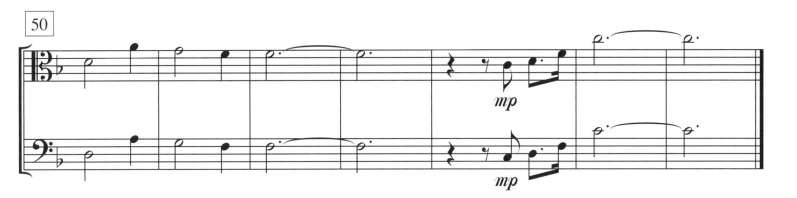

Jesus, Draw Me Close

Viola / Cello / String Bass
ENSEMBLE

Music by **RICK FOUNDS**
Arranged by **STAN PETHEL**

Jesus, Draw Me Close

Viola / Cello / String Bass
SOLO

Music by **RICK FOUNDS**
Arranged by **STAN PETHEL**

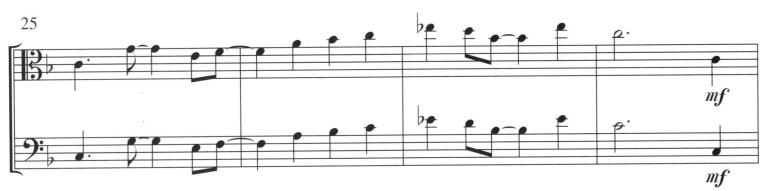

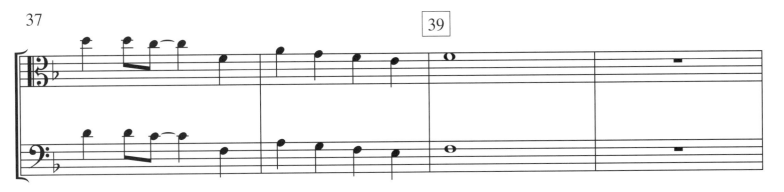

Lord, I Lift Your Name on High

Viola / Cello / String Bass
ENSEMBLE

Music by **RICK POUNDS**
Arranged by **STAN PETHEL**

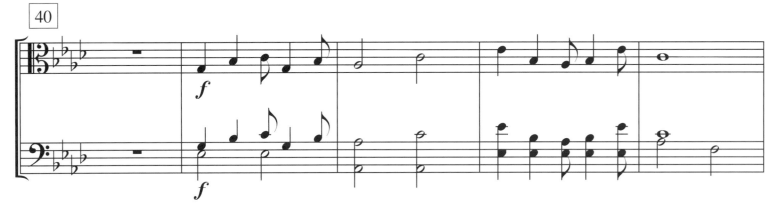

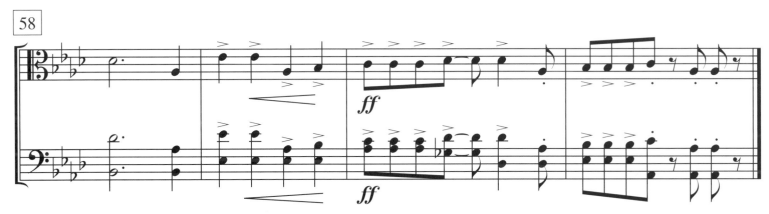

Lord, I Lift Your Name on High

Viola / Cello / String Bass
SOLO

Music by **RICK POUNDS**
Arranged by **STAN PETHEL**

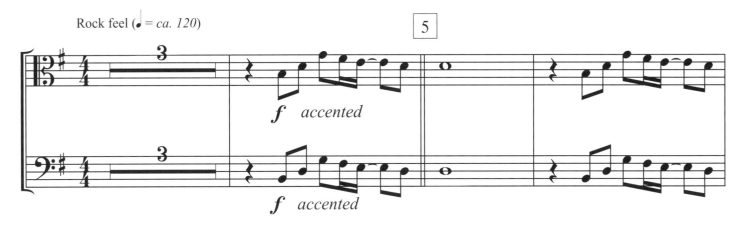

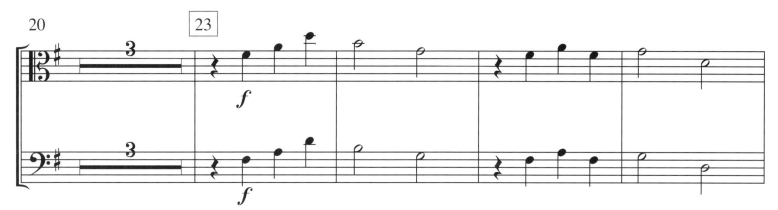

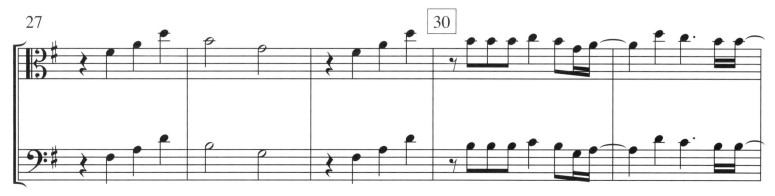

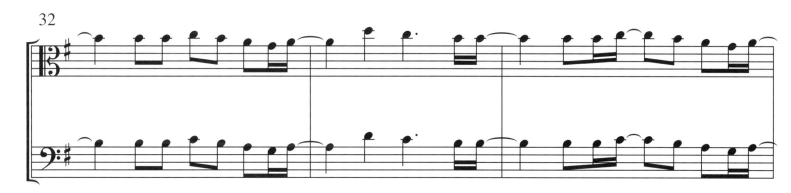

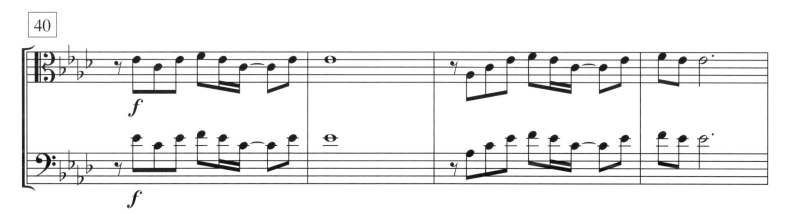

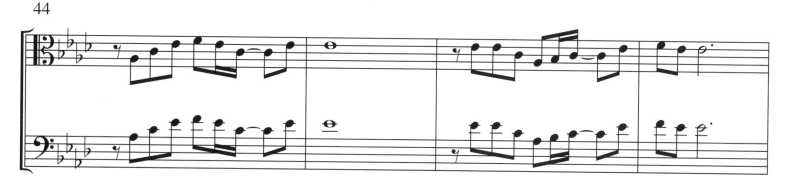

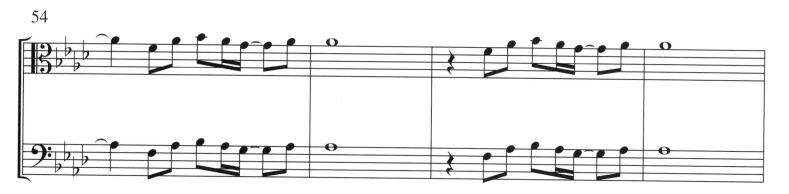

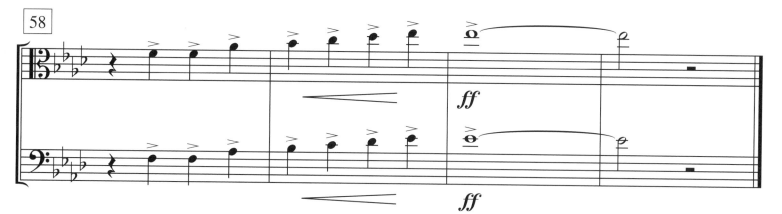

Sanctuary

Viola / Cello / String Bass
ENSEMBLE

Music by **JOHN W. THOMPSON**
and **RANDY SCRUGGS**
Arranged by **STAN PETHEL**

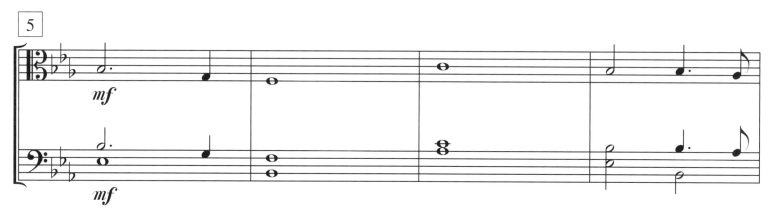

Sanctuary

Viola / Cello / String Bass
SOLO

Music by **JOHN W. THOMPSON**
and **RANDY SCRUGGS**
Arranged by **STAN PETHEL**

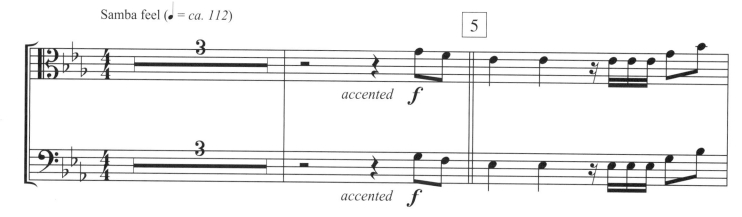

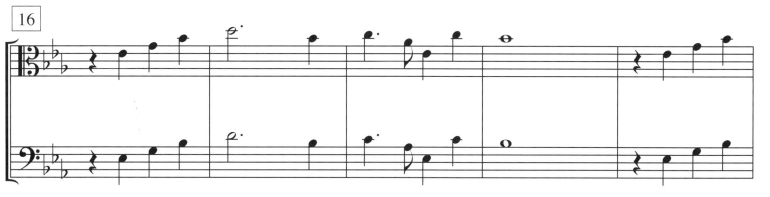

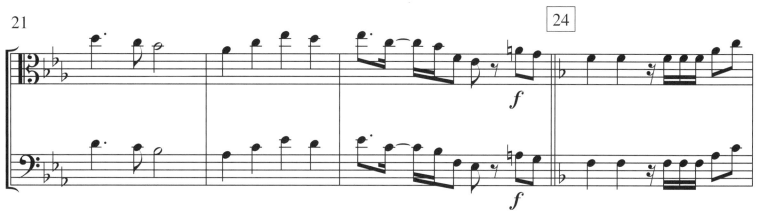

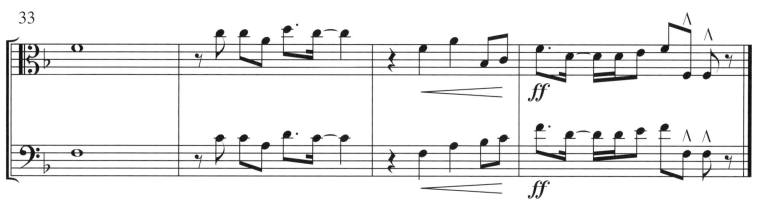

Shine, Jesus, Shine

Viola / Cello / String Bass
ENSEMBLE

Music by **GRAHAM KENDRICK**
Arranged by **STAN PETHEL**

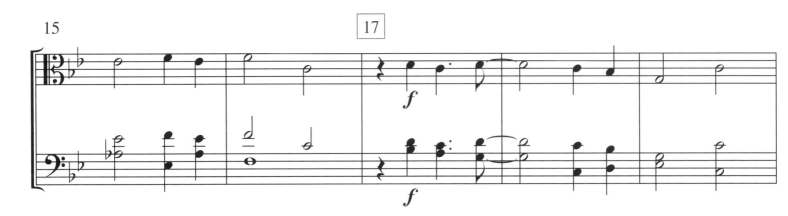

20

25

30

35　　36

40

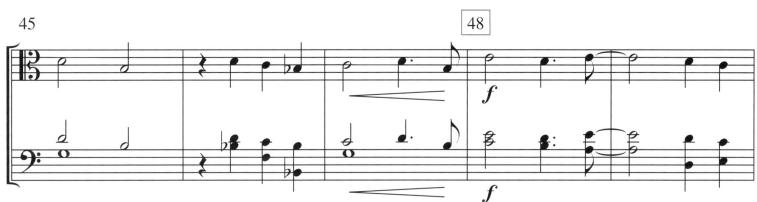

Shine, Jesus, Shine

Viola / Cello / String Bass
SOLO

Music by **GRAHAM KENDRICK**
Arranged by **STAN PETHEL**

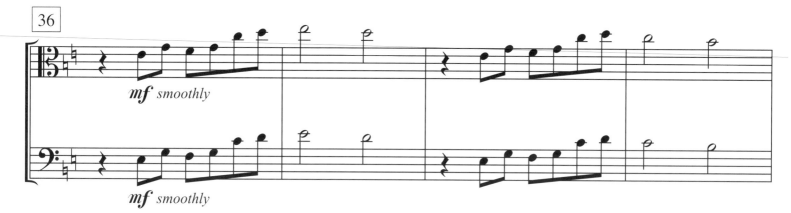

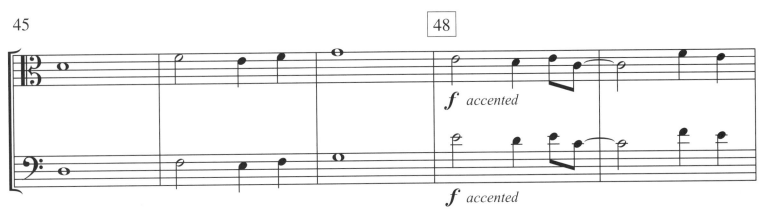

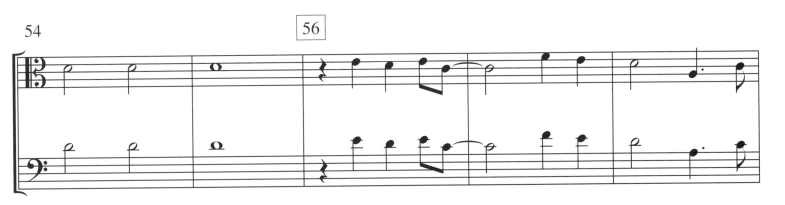

You Are My All In All

Viola / Cello / String Bass
ENSEMBLE

Music by **DENNIS JERNIGAN**
Arranged by **STAN PETHEL**

With an underlying beat (♩ = *ca. 72*)

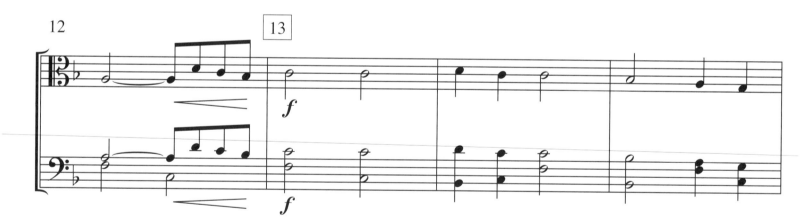

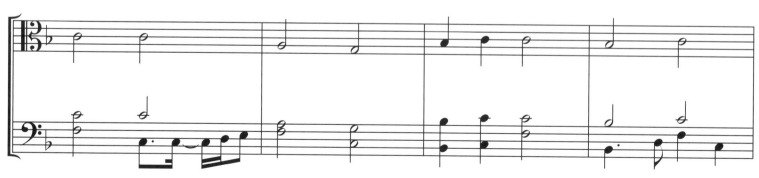

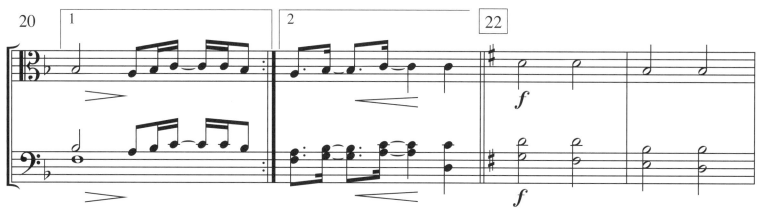

You Are My All In All

Viola / Cello / String Bass
SOLO

Music by **DENNIS JERNIGAN**
Arranged by **STAN PETHEL**

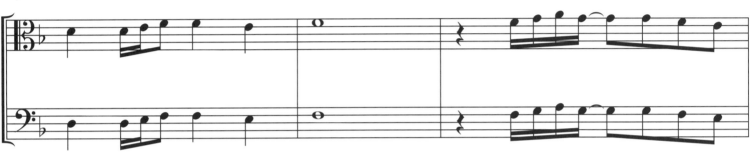

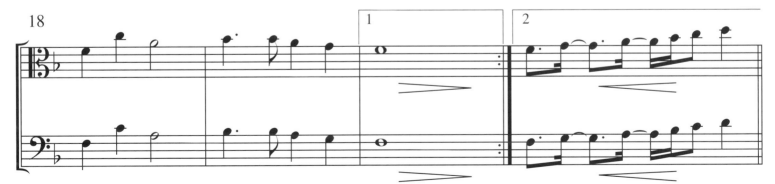

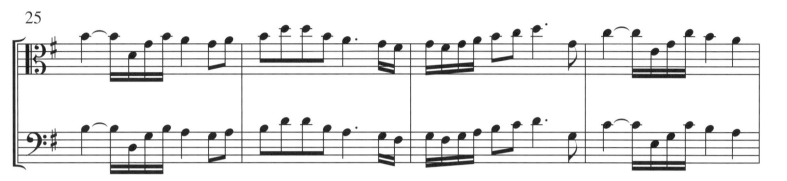